I0755007

DEALING WITH...
HEALTH ISSUES
Mitchell Lane
PUBLISHERS
AIMEE POPALIS

Parent and Caregiver Tips for Creating Nonfiction Readers

Timely topics in the *Dealing With...* series will interest intermediate and middle school readers and equip them with helpful strategies for coping with difficult situations. Your reader will be introduced to new concepts, facts, ideas, and vocabulary.

Tips for Reading Nonfiction

Talk about Nonfiction

Explain that nonfiction books provide facts about real-world topics. When readers read nonfiction, they gain a rich understanding of the world. They build background knowledge that provides a foundation for learning and academic success.

Look at the Parts

This book contains the following helpful features. Share the purpose of each feature with your reader.

Photos, Captions, and Graphic Aids
The photos, captions, charts, and other graphic aids in nonfiction texts contain a wealth of information. Help your reader identify different ways information can be displayed.

Sidebars
These extra tidbits of information help satisfy readers' curiosity and expand their knowledge.

Table of Contents
Located at the front of the book, this list shows the big ideas within the text and the page numbers where they can be found.

Extension Activities and Additional Resources
A "Your Turn" quiz and "Exploration and Discovery" activities invite readers to apply their new knowledge. Supporting resources are provided in a special "You Are Not Alone" section.

Glossary
Located at the back of the book, the glossary defines key words and phrases that are related to the topic. These words and phrases can be found in the text in **bold** type.

Index
Located at the back of the book, the index is an alphabetical list of topics and the page numbers where they can be found.

With a little help and guidance, your reader will be on their way to enjoying and learning from nonfiction books.

Mitchell Lane
PUBLISHERS
mitchelllanepub.com

2001 SW 31st Avenue
Hallandale, FL 33009

First Edition, 2026.
Author: Aimee Popalis
Designer: Rhea Magaro
Editor: Kim Thompson

Series: Dealing With...
Title: Dealing with Health Issues / by Aimee Popalis

Hallandale, FL : Mitchell Lane Publishers, [2026]

Library bound ISBN: 979-8-89260-674-5
eBook ISBN: 979-8-89260-679-0

PHOTO CREDITS
Dreamstime: Sunlight19, 6, 7; Shutterstock: Prostock-studio, cover, 1, 9; imtmphoto, 5; Lukman Haryanto, 8, 33; PeopleImages.com - Yuri A, 10, 19, 34; amedeoemaja, 11; Vector_Up, 13; New Africa, 14, 47; KomootP, 14; Monkey Business Images, 16, 23; Studio Romantic, 17, 32; Lordn, 18; Blueastro, 19; Thongchai S, 20; pics five, 21; Daisy Daisy, 22; Africa Studio, 24; Vitalii Vodolazskyi, 25; tashmetova808, 26; Ground Picture, 27; tajuddin2002bd, 28; originalpunkt, 29; Pixel-Shot, 30; vectorfusionart, 31; Oleksii Synelnykov, 35; Alex Gorka, 36; Rawpixel.com, 37; Elena Elisseeva, 38; Diego Cervo, 39; imtmphoto, 41; iofoto, 42; Ljupco Smokovski, 44

Table of Contents

Chapter 1: Under the Surface

Lucas

Lucas loved to play basketball. He practiced with his dad every weekend, dribbling and shooting for hours. But at school, things felt different. His classmates were friendly enough, but no one ever asked him to play during gym class or on the playground. He didn't feel brave enough to join in on his own.

Lucas knew that his **paralyzed** arm made him stand out. Some kids probably assumed he couldn't even play basketball. He wanted to prove them wrong, but he worried. *What if they laugh at me?* he thought. *What if they take it easy on me or don't pass me the ball?*

What Do You Think?

- Why might Lucas's classmates leave him out? Do you think they intend to hurt his feelings?
- Has a health issue ever made you feel different or left out?
- What could Lucas do to overcome his worries?

Amara

"Amara? Amara, are you listening?"

Amara looked up at her coach, feeling guilty. She hadn't been paying attention. Now, practice was almost over. She felt shaky and unable to continue swimming.

Lately, Amara couldn't stop worrying about getting sick again. Last year, she had to miss the whole swimming season. This year, she was healthy. But her worries were making her feel tired and **distracted**. *What if her illness came back?* she worried. *What if it was worse this time?*

What Do You Think?

- Why might being at swim practice make Amara worry?
- What could Amara do to feel less distracted?
- How does worrying about something make you feel?

Chapter 2: What Are Health Issues?

A health issue is anything that affects how your body or mind feels and works. Health issues often begin with **symptoms**, or signals from your body that something isn't right.

A symptom might be a cough, a stomachache, or constant tiredness. A doctor or health professional can **diagnose** the problem. Then, the doctor can **prescribe** a treatment like medicine, surgery, or **therapy**.

Did You Know?
Health comes from the Latin word *hale*, which means "whole or sturdy." *Healthy* describes something that works well, like a *healthy* environment, relationship, or economy.

Many people think that being healthy means living without illness or injury. But good health is more than that. Being healthy means feeling good in your body and your mind. It means having positive relationships with yourself and others. Health is about feeling happy, strong, and capable of living well.

Types of Health Issues

Health issues can occur at any time in life. Some are present at birth, and some develop over time. Some health issues result from accidents and injuries.

Health problems can last for a short time or persist for a long time. Many can be cured. **Chronic** conditions can be treated or managed, but they do not go away.

Sometimes, a health issue is **terminal**. It cannot be cured or managed. A terminal illness is **fatal** and eventually leads to death. In these cases, doctors and family members focus on making sure the person is comfortable and well cared for.

Did You Know?

A health issue may also be called a:

- Medical condition
- Illness
- Health problem
- Sickness
- Disease
- Health challenge
- Disorder

Health issues come in many forms and affect different parts of the body and mind. Most fit into these main categories. Some conditions fit into more than one category.

Cardiovascular Diseases

These affect the heart and blood vessels. They make it difficult for blood to pump through the body.

*Examples: **congenital** heart defects, rheumatic heart disease*

Chronic Diseases

These are long-lasting health problems. They affect people for months or years.

Examples: sickle cell anemia, eczema, Crohn's disease

Developmental Differences

These affect the way a person learns, thinks, moves, communicates, or experiences the world.

Examples: dyslexia, dyspraxia, autism spectrum disorder (ASD)

Genetic Disorders

These occur when a person's DNA or genetic code affects the way their body works.

Examples: down syndrome, cystic fibrosis, muscular dystrophy

Infectious Diseases

These spread from person to person. They happen when someone comes into contact with a virus, bacteria, fungus, or parasite. They are transmitted by humans, animals, food, or water.

Examples: strep throat, COVID-19, salmonella

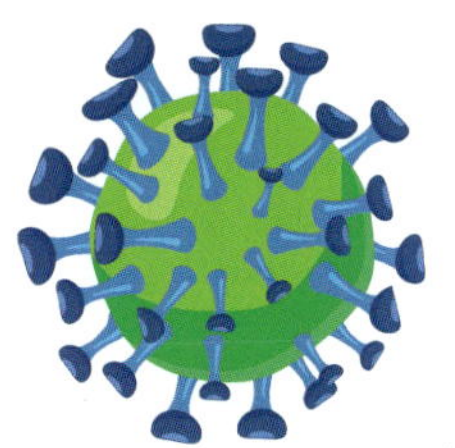

Injuries

These happen when parts of the body get hurt during accidents or as a result of people's activities.

Examples: broken bone, sprain, concussion

Mental Health Disorders

These affect people's emotional or mental well-being. They make it harder to manage behaviors or feelings.

Examples: eating disorders, obsessive-compulsive disorder (OCD)

Neurological Disorders

These affect the brain, nerves, or spine. They can make it difficult to move, learn, or do everyday activities.

Examples: epilepsy, migraine headaches, Tourette's syndrome

Nutritional Disorders

These happen when the body does not get the right amount of nutrients, including vitamins and minerals. They make people feel weak and tired.

Examples: obesity, iron deficiency anemia, vitamin D deficiency

Respiratory Diseases

These affect the lungs. They cause coughing, wheezing, and shortness of breath.

Examples: asthma, bronchitis, pneumonia

Preventing Health Issues

Some health issues can't be avoided, but others can be prevented by practicing healthy habits. Your **immune system** works hard to fight off germs that might make you sick. You can help your immune system function well by eating nutritious food, getting enough sleep, and exercising.

Many injuries are preventable. Wearing a seatbelt and using sports safety gear are easy ways to stay safe.

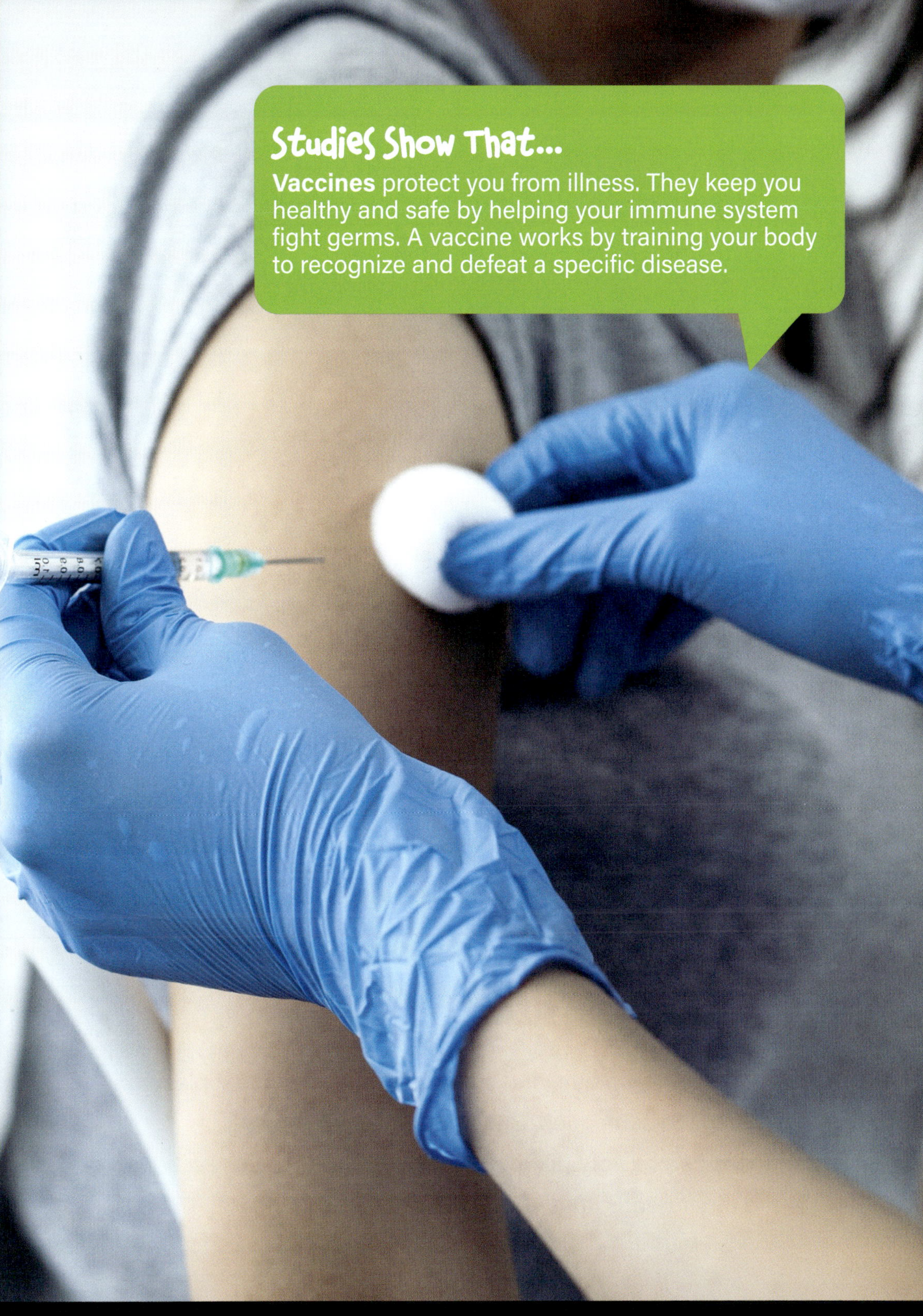

Studies Show That...

Vaccines protect you from illness. They keep you healthy and safe by helping your immune system fight germs. A vaccine works by training your body to recognize and defeat a specific disease.

Health Issues and Individual Differences

Every person is unique, and so is their health. Two people might be allergic to the same food. But if they eat the food, their experiences can be very different. One may have a mild reaction while the other needs immediate, lifesaving treatment.

It is important to remember that different people face different health challenges. Things that some people take for granted, like the ability to climb steps, might be very difficult for others. It is always best to treat others with kindness and **compassion**.

Did You Know?

About one in six kids has a mental health disorder or developmental difference. These health issues occur in every part of the world and affect children of all backgrounds.

Health Issues and the Brain

Your brain and body are connected. The way your body feels impacts your brain and vice versa. When you are sick, or when someone close to you is having health issues, you often feel **stress**. Your brain causes the release of cortisol, a **hormone** that prepares your body to deal with danger. In emergencies, cortisol can be helpful. But over time, it affects your memory and focus. It can slow down healing or lead to serious mental problems like anxiety or depression.

Did You Know?

Your brain has neuroplasticity. That means it can learn, adapt, and change. Practicing healthy habits makes your brain stronger and improves its ability to handle challenges.

Happy Brain Chemistry

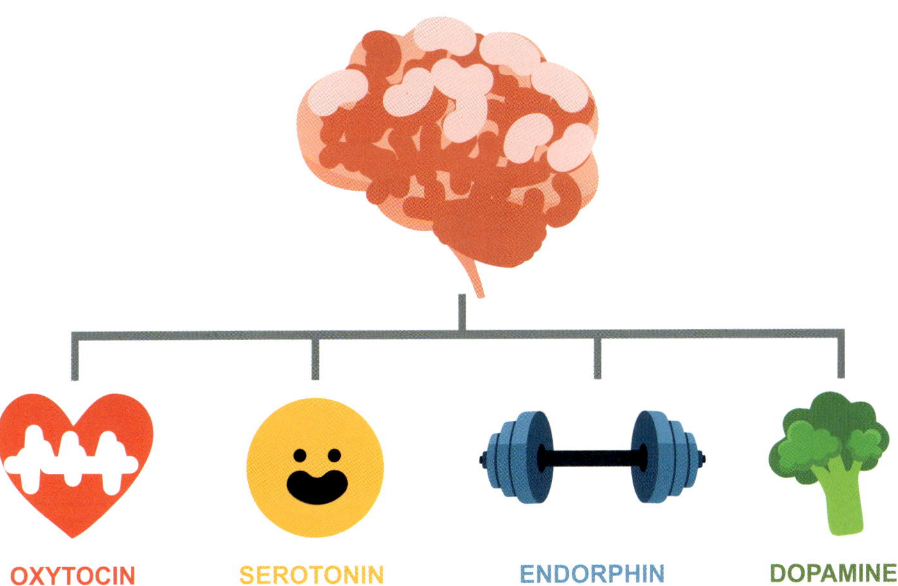

The good news is that caring for your body helps your brain stay happy and strong! Healthy food provides important nutrients for your brain. Sleep helps your brain recover and strengthens your memory. Staying active, even in small ways, helps your brain release hormones called **endorphins**. Endorphins improve your mood and help you manage stress.

Chapter 3: Health Issues and You

Having an illness or injury can present major challenges for individuals and families. Health issues can get in the way of ordinary routines and activities. They can make it hard for kids to attend school, for adults to go to work, and for everyday chores to get done. It takes patience and flexibility to adjust.

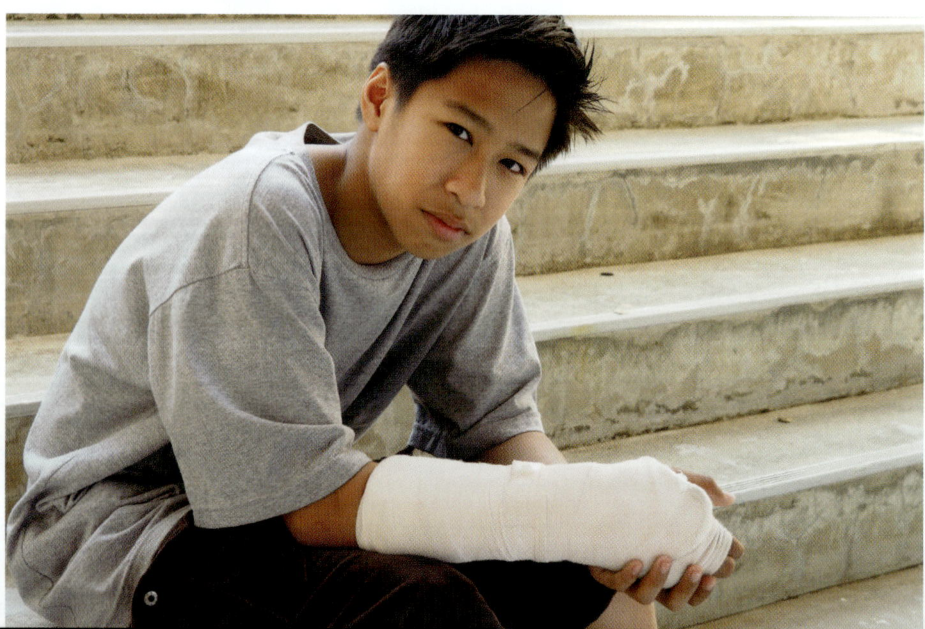

Caring for Yourself

You know your own body, so trust your instincts. Pay attention to signs that something is not quite right with your health. Talk to your parents or a trusted adult even if you feel embarrassed or worried. They can help you understand what's happening and get the treatment you need.

Everyone gets sick or injured from time to time. When you don't feel well, you aren't up to doing much. It helps to remember that healing takes time. Other things can wait while you rest and recover.

When health issues bring changes to your life, it is normal to be upset for a while. There may be small disappointments like missing a party or sporting event. There may be big adjustments like taking daily medication or learning to use a wheelchair. In cases like these, it is understandable to feel frustrated or sad or to think that things are unfair.

Health issues can make it hard to do things you enjoy, like playing a sport or going to school. Sometimes, you'll need to find new ways to do these activities. That's okay! With creativity and determination, you will find options that work for you.

Did You Know?

If you need to stay in the hospital, bring a few items from home to make you more comfortable.

- ☐ Cozy pajamas and a robe or sweatshirt
- ☐ A soft pillow, blanket, or stuffed animal
- ☐ Books, puzzles, or card games
- ☐ A notebook and pens
- ☐ Headphones and a tablet, e-reader, or smartphone
- ☐ Your toothbrush, toothpaste, hairbrush, and shampoo
- ☐ Fidget toys like slime or magic sand

It can feel uncomfortable when people pay too much attention to your health. They may stare, make comments, or think you can't do things that you really can do. This is called **discrimination**, and it is not okay. If this happens, tell an adult you trust.

Most people want to help. It's okay to tell them what you need or how you'd like to be treated. You get to decide how much to say about your health. You can share a lot or a little. Your family members and doctor can help you decide.

If you're worrying a lot, struggling in school, avoiding friends, or losing sleep, talk to a trusted adult. These may be signs that your health issue is affecting your mental health. Taking care of your feelings is just as important as taking care of your body.

There IS Good News!

There are laws that protect people with health issues and make sure they get fair treatment. These laws help everyone get the support they need. They promote equal opportunities for everyone.

Caring for Others

When a friend or family member is unwell, there are many ways to help. You can send a cheerful video message to a relative or do a few extra chores around the house. You can take missed homework assignments to a classmate or carry a friend's backpack while they use crutches.

Sometimes, a loved one's health issues are serious or last for a long time. It can be easy to feel helpless or **overwhelmed**. In these cases, it is important to remember your own needs. Keep to your normal routine as much as possible. Make time for friends and for activities you enjoy. Find a trusted adult who can answer your questions and provide support.

Chapter 4: Strategies for Taking Control

You can't control everything about your health. But focusing on things that you can do makes a big difference. Try these strategies to help you feel your best.

Strategy #1: Be Mindful

Practicing **mindfulness** helps you feel calmer and less worried. It lowers stress, helps you relax, and brings your focus to the present. Try these exercises.

Get Outside

Go outdoors. Walk or sit in a place that lets you see the sky, a tree, or another part of nature. Then, focus on your senses. Notice sounds, smells, and the feel of the air. Leave your phone behind and enjoy each moment as it comes.

Body Scan

1. Find a quiet place to sit or lie down. Gently close your eyes.
2. Take a few slow, deep breaths.
3. Focus on your feet and notice how they feel. Let them relax.
4. Move your attention to your lower legs and knees and notice how they feel. Let them relax.
5. Continue up to your thighs, belly, chest, neck, head, shoulders, arms, and hands. Notice and relax each part.
6. If you feel any tightness or pain, take a deep breath. Imagine the pain melting away as you breathe out.
7. Take a few more deep breaths. When you're ready, open your eyes.

Strategy #2: Connect with Others

When facing a health issue, spending time with people you love makes you feel supported and cared for. It releases those feel-good hormones that lower stress and boost your mood.

Remember that you are not alone. Seek out others who are dealing with the same issues and who can truly understand how you feel. Sharing your worries or successes can make you feel braver and more hopeful. With your parents' help, look for support groups, online forums, or organizations to join.

There IS Good News!

To support someone facing a health issue, try these tips.

- Listen without giving advice or sharing your own stories.
- Accept their feelings without judgment.
- Offer help with tasks, big or small.
- Check in regularly, not just at first.
- Offer kindness and support, not pity.

Strategy #3: Learn the Facts

Learning about your health issues helps you feel more in control. When you understand the facts, you worry less and make better decisions. Avoid internet searches. Instead, talk to your doctor or a trusted adult and ask questions. You can ask things like *How will this help me?* or *What are the options?* Listen carefully to the answers. Ask follow-up questions to make sure you understand. Remember, knowledge is power!

Once you have good information, you can help make choices about your own health care. Discuss your goals and concerns with your family and doctors. Then, speak up about what will help you feel better inside and out.

Studies Show That...

People who recognize that they are in control of their health decisions have better mental and physical health than those who believe that decisions are out of their control.

Strategy #4: Stay Positive

Having a positive outlook is an important part of dealing with a health issue. Expecting good things will help you feel happier and stronger. Studies show that thinking positively can even help your body heal faster! Try these exercises.

Affirmations

Your words have power! Affirmations are short positive statements you say to yourself. They can help you stay positive even when facing health challenges. Use affirmations such as *I am strong* or *I can handle this*. Repeating the words will remind you that you are brave and capable.

Gratitude

Gratitude means being thankful for the good things in your life, no matter how small. Write down three things you're thankful for, like beautiful weather, a favorite snack, or a funny moment with a friend. Be sure to include why you are thankful for each thing. Focusing on things that are going well can help you feel happier even when times are tough.

Studies Show That...

Gratitude has many benefits! It can:

- Help your brain focus on good things
- Boost your energy and mood
- Strengthen your friendships
- Help you stay strong during tough times
- Improve your sleep

Strategy #5: Celebrate Your Success

Celebrating your successes is a powerful way to manage health issues. Reaching even small goals can boost your energy and mood. Try these exercises.

Set Goals

Setting goals is a great way to stay positive. Goals can be small, like taking your medicine on time. They can be big, like playing a sport for the first time after an injury. Reaching goals makes you feel proud and in control.

Set an Intention

Goals focus on the future, but intentions can help you right now. Before an activity, set an intention. Let it guide your actions and choices. You might set an intention to enjoy a meal with your family. You might set an intention to stay calm and ask questions during a doctor appointment. Intentions help you feel in control and make the most of each moment.

Celebrate!

Celebrate every achievement, big or small! Reward yourself with a sticker, a treat, or extra time doing something you love. Share your success with friends and family too. Celebrating acknowledges your hard work and keeps you motivated. You can accomplish great things!

Strategy #6: Practice Self-Care

Taking good care of yourself is one of the best ways to deal with and prevent health issues. You can develop healthy habits that support your body and mind. Try these exercises.

Self-Compassion Break

Life is full of challenges, including health challenges. Take a self-compassion break to help yourself through tough moments.

1. Recognize that this moment is stressful.
2. Accept that stress and suffering are a part of life.
3. Ask, "What can I do or say to be kind to myself right now?"

Express Yourself

Creating something helps you feel happy, relaxed, and good about yourself! Drawing, painting, and writing are fun ways to express yourself. Try doodling, coloring, or writing a story. The process of creating is more important than the product you make.

Chapter 5: Dealing with Health Issues

Remember Amara? Her coach handed her a small card with a breathing exercise on it. "Try this," she said. "It's called mindfulness. It really helps me when I feel overwhelmed."

Amara followed the steps on the card. She focused on her breath. In and out. Afterward, she felt better. Her worry hadn't completely gone away, but now she had a tool to help calm it. She felt hopeful that she could manage both her physical and mental health.

Amara's coach checked in with her at the end of practice. "Feeling better?" she asked.

Amara nodded and smiled. "Yes," she said. "See you tomorrow!"

Remember Lucas? One day, he got tired of watching from the sidelines. He decided to speak up. "Hey, can I play?" he asked, trying to sound confident.

The other kids exchanged glances. "Sure," one of them finally said.

Lucas took a deep breath and joined the game. He dodged defenders and made passes. Because of his paralyzed arm, his moves looked a bit different. But that just meant he played his own way. When he scored, his new teammates cheered.

Finally, Lucas understood that what he did with his abilities mattered far more than his disability.

Remember: Your health doesn't define who you are or what you can do. Stay positive. You are strong and capable, no matter what!

YOUR TURN: HOW DO YOU DEAL WITH HEALTH ISSUES?

For each situation, select the answer most likely to produce the best outcome. Make a note of your answers on a separate sheet of paper.

1. Xavier finds it hard to remember to do his physical therapy exercises for his injury. How can Xavier stay on top of his recovery?
   - **A.** Skip the exercises because they're too much trouble...and they're uncomfortable.
   - **B.** Set up a reminder system to help him remember.
   - **C.** Learn more about why the exercises are helpful and reward himself each time he completes them.

2. Eva has epilepsy. She feels embarrassed about her seizures, so she doesn't want her friends to know. How can Eva avoid being embarrassed?
   - **A.** Join a support group to get advice on talking to friends about epilepsy.
   - **B.** Avoid her friends and make excuses to hide her seizures.
   - **C.** Write in a journal and draw to express her feelings.

3. Harrison was just diagnosed with a severe allergy. He is feeling worried and scared. How can Harrison feel calm and comfortable again?
   - **A.** Regularly check with his parents and teachers to ensure things are safe and avoid new places and situations entirely.
   - **B.** Try mindfulness exercises when his worries become overwhelming.
   - **C.** Ignore his allergy and hope nothing happens.

4. Jasmine has started getting headaches and blurry vision. What should she do about her new symptoms?
   - **A.** Ignore her symptoms and hope they go away.
   - **B.** Focus on eating well, staying active, and getting enough sleep.
   - **C.** Talk to her parents about her headaches and changes in her eyesight.

Think about your answers.

1. The best answer is C. Having a better understanding of his exercises can help Xavier see the purpose of completing them. Remembering to celebrate afterward will motivate him and make doing his exercises more enjoyable.
2. The best answer is A. Joining a support group can help Eva get past her embarrassment and understand that many people face the same challenges. Finding ways to communicate with her friends will also help her feel less alone and more supported.
3. The best answer is B. Mindfulness exercises can help Harrison manage his worries when they arise and feel calm and in control.
4. The best answer is C. Talking to her parents will help Jasmine get the support she needs to see a doctor and get a diagnosis for her headaches and vision changes.

EXPLORATION AND DISCOVERY: ACTIVITIES TO TRY

1. Make a self-care menu. Write a list of activities that you enjoy, such as listening to music, baking, or petting your dog. Aim to do at least one of these activities each day for a week. Regularly choosing something from your menu will help you feel cared for and healthy.
2. Write a letter to your body. Express all the things you appreciate about it. Ask it questions. Share your wishes and hopes for all the things your body will do. Finish by listing some steps you will take to care for yourself and help your body feel its best.
3. Find a health hero. Draw or write about someone who overcame a health challenge. It could be someone you know, a celebrity, or a historical figure. Share what you learn with others.
4. Do something that helps others. Consider volunteering at an animal shelter, reading to nursing home residents, or assisting a neighbor. Small acts of kindness can make a big difference and make you feel good!

YOU ARE NOT ALONE

Experiencing health issues can make you feel hopeless and alone. But you are NOT alone. There are good people who care about you and want to help. There are also many resources you can use to learn more and help yourself.

Explore some of these ways to find the kindness and support you deserve.

People to Ask for Help

☑ guidance counselor
☑ teacher
☑ principal
☑ assistant principal
☑ parent
☑ older sibling
☑ grandparent
☑ aunt or uncle
☑ coach
☑ school secretary
☑ bus driver
☑ religious youth group leader
☑ any friend that you trust
☑ any adult that you trust

Websites

National Alliance on Mental Illness: Kids, Teens, and Young Adults
www.nami.org/your-journey/kids-teens-and-young-adults
Learn more about mental health, locate resources, and find support.

National Heart, Blood, and Lung Institute: Materials to Share with Children and Teens
www.nhlbi.nih.gov/health/educational/wecan/tools-resources/child-teen-resources.htm
Discover fun facts about your heart and lungs and activities you can do to keep them healthy.

Nemours TeensHealth: Mind
kidshealth.org/en/teens/your-mind
Explore this collection of resources for a healthy mind and body.

Books

Burnell, Cerrie. *I Am Not a Label: 34 Disabled Artists, Thinkers, Athletes and Activists from Past and Present.* Wide Eyed Editions, 2020.

McDunn, Gillian. *Honestly Elliott.* Bloomsbury Children's Books, 2023.

Silva, Cassie. *Listening to the Quiet.* Lantana Publishing, 2023.

Phone Helplines

Crisis Text Line
Text HOME to 741741 or message on WhatsApp. Young people of color can text STEVE to 741741 to reach culturally trained counselors.

LGBT National Youth Talkline
1-800-246-7743

National Suicide Prevention Lifeline
1-800-273-8255

Suicide and Crisis Lifeline
Call or text 988.

GLOSSARY

chronic (KRAH-nik)
Lasting for a long time or returning

compassion (kuhm-PASH-uhn)
A feeling of sympathy for someone who is suffering

congenital (kuhn-JE-nuh-tuhl)
Existing at birth

diagnose (dye-uhg-NOHS)
To determine what disease a patient has or figure out what is causing a problem

discrimination (dis-krim-i-NAY-shuhn)
Unfair treatment of someone because they are different

distracted (di-STRAK-tuhd)
Unable to concentrate or pay attention

endorphins (en-DOR-finz)
Chemicals released in your body that dull pain and improve mood

fatal (FAY-tuhl)
Causing or leading to death

hormone (HOR-mone)
A chemical made by the body that affects growth, development, and behavior

immune system (i-MYOON SIS-tuhm)
The body's defense against germs and sickness

mindfulness (MINDE-fuhl-nis)
The practice of focusing your attention on the present moment

overwhelmed (oh-vur-WELMD)
Overpowered by thoughts, feelings, and demands; having a strong emotional response to circumstances

paralyzed (PAR-uh-lized)
Unable to move or function

prescribe (pri-SKRIBE)
To recommend a specific kind of medication or treatment

stress (stres)
Worry, strain, or pressure

symptoms (SIMP-tuhmz)
Signs and indications that something is happening or that something is a problem

terminal (TUR-muh-nuhl)
Unable to cure and leading to death

therapy (THER-uh-pee)
A treatment for an illness, injury, or mental issue

vaccines (vak-SEENZ)
Medical treatments that help a person's body defend itself from infections

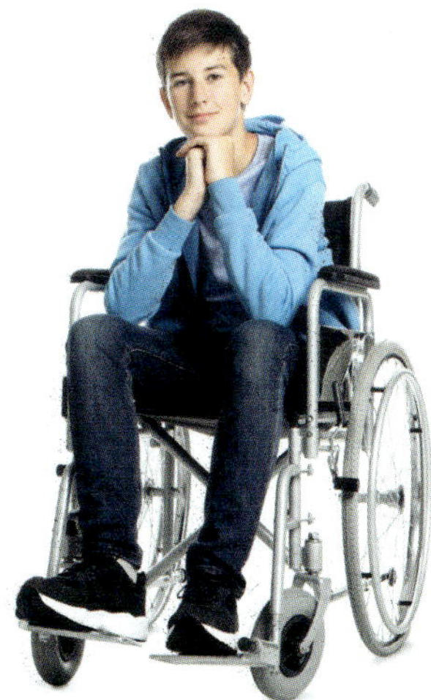

INDEX

ABOUT THE AUTHOR

Aimee Popalis is a mom and super-fun science teacher from Tampa, Florida. When she is not exploring with her students or hiking with her family, she loves writing books that help kids better understand the world around them. At home, she's helping her dog adapt to a life with food allergies—no more leftover pancakes! Aimee knows that anyone, human or animal, can tackle obstacles with the right support and a little creativity. Through this book, she hopes to share helpful strategies and lots of encouragement for kids facing health changes and challenges.